We
Love Our
Country

America's Constitutional Republic

Mary L. Amlaw

Fourth Printing - 2012

ISBN-10:   0-615-36482-9
ISBN-13: 978-0-615-36482-7

Cover illustration: Microsoft Office Online Clip Art
Illustrations not sourced: Microsoft Office Online Clip Art and
www.Ace-Clipart.com

www.WeLoveOurCountryOnline.com

Bulk discount available for instruction or fundraising

For more information, contact us at
WeLoveOurCountry@gmail.com

Table of Contents

"The name of American, which belongs to you...must always exalt the just pride of Patriotism..."

George Washington
Farewell Address, September 17, 1796
http://www.marksquotes.com/Founding-Fathers/GeorgeWashingtonQuotes

"Every difference of opinion is not a difference of principle."

Thomas Jefferson
First Inaugural Address, March 4, 1801
http://www.marksquotes.com/Founding-Fathers/ThomasJeffersonQuotes

Preface

Our Founding Fathers hoped we would always follow the principles our Country were founded upon. They include the equal right to opportunity to live to our potential and to achieve personal happiness, free to choose and associate as a result of limited governmental influence, and to own and enjoy property in a moral and civil society that upholds equal treatment under established laws. All are based on principles derived from Natural Law *("...to which the laws of nature and of nature's God entitle them...")*, and we are never to give to government any power or rights that we do not personally possess.

When we live by Founding principles, we think and behave in terms of being American.

Not as party affiliation.

Not as special interest.

Not as minority or majority.

Not as liberal or conservative, left or right.

But as American. Sharing and protecting the same principles.

Introduction

Based on the writings of our Founding Fathers, I provide a short, simple, and organized explanation of the natural rights we have as human beings and as Americans, of our Constitutional Republic government, and of the responsibility American citizens have to support and preserve the Constitution of the United States of America that protects our rights and freedoms.

The book is for ages seven through adult to learn more accurately, and to appreciate the timeless relevance of, our Country's Declaration of Independence and Constitution. The book may also be used as a speaker outline as well as an instructional tool by parents, teachers, and religious and organizational leaders.

As reference material, the book contains applicable quotes of our first five Presidents who were Founding Fathers, the above Founding documents, the Bill of Rights, the Pledge of Allegiance, and the founding Principles of Liberty. A basic understanding of Natural Law, human nature, a Republic versus a Democracy form of government, and free market versus controlled market economic systems also help in discussing the content of the book.

As a united, assimilated, and knowledgeable Nation, we are Americans following the Founding values and principles of our Country. Doing so preserves our rights and freedoms, promotes individual and societal civility, safety and prosperity, provides clearly defined voting criteria, and enables us to recognize any movement contrary to the original intent of our Constitution.

Mary L. Amlaw

"Children should be educated and instructed in the principles of freedom."

John Adams
Defense of the Constitutions of Government
of the United States, 1787

http://www.constitution.org/jadams

"A well-instructed people alone can be permanently a free people."

James Madison
Virginia State Convention Speech, December 5, 1810

http://www.creativequotations.com/Search/James Madison

Donated by

Republican Women of Prescott

In Memory of

Miriam Kuebler

Our Country is the United States of America

And we love our Country because it was created with knowledge that everyone is born with natural rights from our Creator. They include the equal right to self-preservation and....

To live

To use abilities

To earn and own property

To use and enjoy what we own

To seek happiness

To be safe from harm

To love and create family

To make choices for our well-being

These rights are universal and necessary to keep the human will and spirit alive. They are derived from Natural Law, or the law of nature as created by God. Because we are born with them, they are permanent and not to be legislated against by any government.

Natural Law is logical, orderly, and moral, and includes who we naturally are as human beings. One of human nature's most defining characteristics is the inability and dislike to be oppressed physically, emotionally, spiritually, and intellectually. Instead, there is ...

> An ability and desire to create and prosper, to change and grow
>
> An ability to recognize fairness
>
> A need to know truths
>
> A need for order and purpose
>
> A desire to earn, own, and keep
>
> A desire to speak and be heard

Our Country's form of Government is a Constitutional Republic

And we love our Country's form of government as it is one that serves and protects us by following written and established laws contained in our Federal Constitution, the Constitution of the United States of America.

These laws are timeless and always relevant as they are based on Natural Law and are intended to protect individual liberty and the right to private property, and economic freedom from any form of government that takes them away.

The laws of our Constitution are not to be ignored or infringed by current opinion or movement, or by those who wish to create a society that does not recognize and honor Natural Law.

Some of our natural rights have been identified in the Bill of Rights, supporting the original intent of the Constitution to protect God-given rights and limit the say of government in our personal lives.

These rights guarantee many freedoms which in order to be maintained are established through self-reliance and knowledge, reflected in opportunity, and preserved by morality and civility. We are free...

> To be knowledgeable and state what we believe and know

> To practice our faith and beliefs

> To peacefully gather to agree and disagree

> To self-govern

> To make private and personal choices

> To better ourselves

> To work and earn and own

> To use and enjoy what we own, choosing to share often

> To pursue our dreams, finding and working towards our own happiness

The laws of our Constitution also protect these freedoms by limiting the power and responsibility of the Federal government. Its role and responsibilities are clearly defined and listed in the Constitution. Limited power protects us from a national government becoming overly-centralized and forceful by legislating against natural rights and personal freedoms, choices and opportunities. Limited power avoids the loss of Natural Law, protects State power, and upholds our individual rights to life, property, safety, justice, and therefore, happiness.

As a Republic, there is a separation of power to protect against oppressive leaders, law-makers, and judges. As a Republic, we elect people to represent us and follow the laws of the Constitution's original intent as well as uphold them when making new laws. Following the laws preserves our Constitutional Republic so we remain free and productive in a safe and prosperous society. Our freedom, opportunity, property, and safety are preserved in their promise by oath…

> To protect our right to worship and communicate, and to know truths from a thorough and unbiased press

> To protect our rights of privacy and equal treatment under Law

> To uphold a free market economic system, the only system that supports Natural Law

and our Republican form of government; to protect our Capitalist economic system of bartering free from government control, and the social system that recognizes the individual's natural right to opportunity, prosperity, and private property

To limit national taxation and indebtedness and to the enumerated powers, and to protect the value of our currency

To provide an unattackable national defense benefiting all citizens

To promote business abroad and ensure the free flow of goods from State to State

We the People
Keep our Country
Free and Prosperous

And we love our Country because it is good and based on laws to protect and empower us.

To preserve the rights and freedoms our Country offers, we have individual and community responsibility...

>To learn what our Founding Fathers knew so we understand the principled reasoning of our Constitution and Country

>To know history so we recognize truths, avoid past errors, and protect our rights

>To defend our rights and freedoms, and to honor the rights and freedoms of others, so we remain moral and law-abiding, upholding Natural Law, thus preserving a civil and safe society

To be productive so we strengthen our and our family's well being as the fundamental basis of community and Country

To rely on one's self, family, and community first to solve problems

To help those truly in need so they are able to contribute to the prosperity and safety of their family, community, and Country

To call ourselves Americans and share our Country's values and principles

To value our self-governing role and be knowledgeable in the law-making process

To vote for honorable representatives who uphold the Constitution's original intent and to replace them when they do not

To honor those who fight, and have fought, to keep our Country free and principled

To respect the Flag that represents the values and principles of our Country

**Our Country is the
United States of America.**

We Love Our Country

Presidential Quotes

George Washington:

"There exists in the economy and course of nature, an indissoluble union between virtue and happiness; between duty and advantage; between the genuine maxims of an honest and magnanimous policy, and the solid rewards of public prosperity and felicity; since we ought to be no less persuaded that the propitious smiles of Heaven can never be expected on a nation that disregards the eternal rules of order and right, which Heaven itself has ordained."

First Inaugural Address,
April 30, 1789
http://www.notablequotes.com/w/washington_george

"Of all the dispositions and habits which lead to political prosperity, religion and morality are indispensable supports."

Farewell Address to the people of the United States,
September 17, 1796
http://www.notablequotes.com/w/washington_george

"...(if) the freedom of speech may be taken away... dumb and silent we may be led, like sheep to the slaughter..."

Address to the officers of the Army,
March 15, 1783
http://www.notablequotes.com/w/washington_george

George Washington
First President of the United States, 1789-1797
George Washington portrait by Rembrandt Peale, www.Library of
Congress.com/GeorgeWashingtonPortrait

"To be prepared for war is one of the most effectual means of preserving peace."

First Annual Address to Congress,
January 8, 1790
http://www.notablequotes.com/w/washington_george

"There is a rank due to the United States, among nations, which will be withheld, if not absolutely lost, by the reputation of weakness. If we desire to avoid insult, we must be able to repel it; if we desire to secure peace, one of the most powerful instruments of our rising prosperity, it must be known that we are at all times ready for war."

Annual Message to Congress,
December 1793
http://www.marksquotes.com/Founding-Fathers/GeorgeWashingtonQuotes

"To contract new debts is not the way to pay old ones."

Letter to James Welch,
April 7, 1799
http://www.notablequotes.com/w/washington_george

"A people… who are possessed of the spirit of commerce, who see and who will pursue their advantages may achieve almost anything."

Letter to Benjamin Harris,
Date unknown
http://www.notable-quotes.com/w/washington_george

"Your love of liberty – your respect for the laws – your habits of industry – and your practice of the moral and religious obligations, are the strongest claims to national and individual happiness."

Letter to the Residents of Boston, October 27, 1789

"…America is open to receive not only the Opulent and respectable strange, but the oppressed and persecuted of all Nations and Religions; whom we shall welcome to a participation of all our rights and privileges if by decency and propriety of conduct they appear to merit the enjoyment."

Letter (recipient unknown), December 2, 1783

"The power of the Constitution will always be in the people. It is entrusted for certain defined purposes, and for a certain limited period to representatives of their own choosing, and when it is executed contrary to their interest or not agreeable to their wishes, their servants can and undoubtedly will be recalled."

Letter to Bushrod Washington, November 10, 1787

John Adams:

"Liberty must at all hazards be supported. We have a right to it, derived from our Maker…"

A Dissertation on the Canon Feudal Law, 1765
http://www.marksquotes.com/Founding-Fathers/JohnAdamsQuotes

"Each individual of the society has a right to be protected by it in the enjoyment of his life, liberty, and property, according to standing laws….But no part of the property of any individual can, with justice, be taken from him or applied to public uses, without his own consent or that of the representative body of the people."

Thoughts on Government, 1776
http://www.marksquotes.com/Founding-Fathers/JohnAdamQuotes

"There is also in human nature a resentment of injury, and indignation against wrong. A love of truth and a veneration of virtue."

The Novanglus, 1775
http://www.marksquotes.com/Founding-Fathers/JohnAdamsQuotes

"Liberty cannot be preserved without a general knowledge among the people, who have a right, from the frame of their nature, to knowledge, as their great Creator…has given them understandings and a desire to know…"

Dissertation on Canon and Feudal Law, 1765
http://www.marksquotes.com/Founding-Fathers/JohnAdamsQuotes

John Adams
Second President of the United States, 1797-1801

John Adams portrait by Asher B. Durand, http://en.wikipedia.org/wiki/JohnAdams

"That, as a republic is the best of governments, so that particular arrangements of the powers of society, or in other words, that form of government which is best contrived to secure an impartial and exact execution of the laws, is the best of republics."

Thoughts on Government, 1776
http://www.marksquotes.com/Founding-Fathers/JohnAdamsQuotes

"The dignity and stability of government in all its branches, the morals of the people, and every blessing of society depend so much upon an upright and skillful administration of justice, that the judicial power ought to be distinct from both the legislative and executive, and independent upon both, that so it may be a check upon both, and both should be checks upon that."

Thoughts on Government, 1776
http://www.marksquotes.com/Founding-Fathers/JohnAdamsQuotes

"They define a republic to be a government of laws, and not of men."

The Novanglus, 1775
http://www.marksquotes.com/Founding-Fathers/JohnAdamsQuotes

"Democracy will soon degenerate into an anarchy, such an anarchy that every man will do what is right in his own eyes and no man's life or property or reputation or liberty will be secure, and every one of these will soon mold itself into a system of subordination of all the moral virtues and intellectual abilities, all the powers of wealth, beauty, wit and science, to the wanton pleasures, the capricious will, and the execrable cruelty of one or a very few."

An Essay on Man's Lust for Power,
August 29, 1763

"The fundamental law of the militia is that it be created, directed and commanded by the laws, and ever for the support of the laws."

A Defense of the Constitutions
of the United States, 1787-1788

"Our Constitution was made only for a moral and religious people. It is wholly inadequate to the government of any other."

Address to the Military,
October 11, 1798

"…Is the duty of all men in society, publicly, and at stated seasons, to worship the Supreme Being, the great Creator and Preserver of the universe."

Thoughts on Government, 1776

"It should be your care, therefore, and mine, to elevate the minds of our children and exalt their courage to accelerate and animate their industry and activity, to excite in them an habitual contempt of meanness, abhorrence of injustice and inhumanity, and an ambition to excel in every capacity, faculty and virtue. If we suffer their minds to grovel and creep in infancy, they will grovel all their lives."

Dissertation on the Canon and Feudal Law, 1756

http://www.marksquotes.com/Founding-Fathers/JohnAdamsQuotes

Thomas Jefferson:

"The God who gave us life, gave us liberty at the same time."

A Summary view of the Rights of British America, 1775
http://lcweb2.loc.gov/Presidents/Jefferson,Thomas/essays/selectedquotations

"The Declaration of Independence...(is the) declaratory charter of our rights, and the rights of man."

Letter to Samuel Adams Wells,
May 12, 1821
http://www.marksquotes.com/Founding-Fathers/ThomasJeffersonQuotes

"A free people (claim) their rights as derived from the laws of nature, and not as the gift of their chief."

Rights of British America, 1774
http://www.marksquotes.com/Founding-Fathers/ThomasJeffersonQuotes

"Natural rights (are) the objects for the protection of which society is formed and municipal laws established."

Letter to James Monroe, 1791
http://www.marksquotes.com/Founding-Fathers/ThomasJeffersonQuotes

"...Equal and justice to all men, of whatever persuasion, religious or political."

First Inaugural Address,
March 4, 1801
http://www.marksquotes.com/Founding-Fathers/ThomasJeffersonQuotes

Thomas Jefferson
Third President of the United States, 1801-1809
Thomas Jefferson portrait by Rembrandt Peale, http://en.wikipedia.org/wiki/ThomasJefferson

"No free man shall ever be debarred the use of firearms within his own lands. The strongest reason for the people to retain the right to keep and bear arms is, as a last resort, to protect themselves against tyranny in government"

Proposal to Virginia's Constitution, 1776
http://lcweb2.loc.gov/Presidents/Jefferson,Thomas/essays/selectedquotations

"The republican is the only form of government which is not eternally at open or secret war with the rights of mankind."

Letter to William Hunter,
March 11, 1790
http://www.marksquotes.com/Founding-Fathers/ThomasJeffersonQuotes

"To preserve the republican form and principles of our Constitution and cleave to the salutary distribution of powers which that (the Constitution) has established...are the two sheet anchors of our Union. If driven from either, we shall be in danger of foundering."

Letter to Judge William Johnson,
June 12, 1823
http://www.marksquotes.com/Founding-Fathers/ThomasJeffersonQuotes

"The whole art of government consists in the art of being honest. Only aim to do your duty, and mankind will give you credit where you fail."

A Summary View of the Rights of British America, 1775
http://www.marksquotes.com/Founding-Fathers/ThomasJeffersonQuotes

"The most sacred of the duties of a government (is) to do equal and impartial justice to all citizens."

Note in Destutte de Tracy, 1816
http://www.marksquotes.com/Founding-Fathers/ThomasJeffersonQuotes

"The constitutions of most of our States assert that all power is inherent in the people; that they may exercise it by themselves in all cases to which they think themselves competent, or they may act by representatives, freely and equally chosen; that it is their right and duty to be at all times armed; that they are entitled to freedom of person, freedom of religion, freedom of property, and freedom of the press."

Letter to John Cartwright, 1824
http://www.marksquotes.com/Founding-Fathers/ThomasJeffersonQuotes

"It would reduce the [Constitution] to a single phrase, that of instituting a Congress with power to do whatever would be for the good of the United States; and as they would be the sole judges of the good or evil, it would be also a power to do whatever evil they please. Certainly no such universal power was meant to be given them. It [the Constitution] was intended to lace them up straightly within the enumerated powers..."

Opinion on a National Bank, 1791
http://PatriotPost.us

"...Banking establishments are more dangerous than standing armies, and that the principle of spending monies to be paid by prosperity, under the name of funding, is but swindling futurity on a large scale."

Letter to John Taylor,
May 28, 1816
http://www.marksquotes.com/Founding-Fathers/ThomasJeffersonQuotes

"The multiplication of public offices, increase of expense beyond income, growth and entailment of a public debt, are indications soliciting the employment of the pruning knife."

Letter to Spencer Roane,
March 9, 1821
http://www.marksquotes.com/Founding-Fathers/ThomasJeffersonQuotes

"We must not let our rulers load us with perpetual debt."

Letter to Samuel Kercheval,
July 12, 1816
http://www.marksquotes.com/Founding-Fathers/ThomasJeffersonQuotes

"I, however, place economy among the first and most important republican virtues, and public debt as the greatest of the dangers to be feared."

Letter to William Plumer,
July 21, 1816
http://lcweb2.loc.gov/Presidents/Jefferson,Thomas/essays/selectedquotations

"Excessive taxation will carry reason and reflection to every man's door, and particularly in the hour of election."

Letter to John Taylor,
November 26, 1798
http://www.marksquotes.com/Founding-Fathers/ThomasJeffersonQuotes

"If we can prevent the government from wasting the labors of the people, under the pretence of taking care of them, they must become happy."

Letter to Thomas Cooper,
November 29, 1802
http://www.marksquotes.com/Founding-Fathers/ThomasJeffersonQuotes

"A wise and frugal government…shall restrain men from injuring one another, shall leave them otherwise free to regulate their own pursuits of industry and government, and shall not take from the mouth of labor the bread it has earned. This is the sum of good government."

First Inaugural Address,
March 4, 1801
http://www.marksquotes.com/Founding-Fathers/ThomasJeffersonQuotes

"To take from one, because it is thought his own industry and that of his fathers has acquired too much, in order to spare to others, who, or whose fathers, have not exercised equal industry and skill, is to violate arbitrarily the first principle of association, the guarantee to everyone the free exercise of his industry and the fruits acquired by it."

Letter to Joseph Milligan,
April 6, 1816
http://www.marksquotes.com/Founding-Fathers/ThomasJeffersonQuotes

"The spirit of resistance to government is so valuable on certain occasions, that I wish it to be always kept alive."

Letter to Abigail Adams,
February 22, 1787
http://www.marksquotes.com/Founding-Fathers/ThomasJeffersonQuotes

"Our liberty depends on the freedom of the press, and that cannot be limited without being lost."

Letter to Dr. James Currie,
January 28, 1789
http://lcweb2.loc.gov/Presidents/Jefferson,Thomas/essays/selectedquotations

"No government ought to be without censors and where the press is free, no one ever will"

Letter to George Washington,
September 9, 1792
http://www.marksquotes.com/Founding-Fathers/ThomasJeffersonQuotes

"Where the press is free and every man able to read, all is safe."

Letter to Charles Yancey,
January 6, 1816
http://www.marksquotes.com/Founding-Fathers/ThomasJeffersonQuotes

"Whenever the people are well informed, they can be trusted with their own government; that whenever things get so far wrong as to attract their notice, they may be relied on to set them to rights."

Letter to Richard Price,
January 8, 1879
http://lcweb2.loc.gov/Presidents/Jefferson, Thomas/essays/selectedquotations

"It is the manners and spirit of a people which preserve a republic in vigor. A degeneracy in these is a canker which soon eats to the heart of its laws and constitution."

Notes on the State of Virginia, Query,   1781
http://www.marksquotes.com/Founding-Fathers/ThomasJeffersonQuotes

"Love your neighbor as yourself and your country more than yourself."

Letter to Thomas Jefferson Smith,
February 21, 1825
http://www.marksquotes.com/Founding-Fathers/ThomasJeffersonQuotes

"On every question of construction, carry ourselves back to the time when the Constitution was adopted, recollect the spirit manifested in the debates and instead of trying what meaning may be squeezed out of the text or invented against it, conform to the probable one in which it was passed."

Letter to William Johnson, 1823
The Jeffersonian Cyclopedia, 1900, page 844

"Agriculture, manufactures, commerce, and navigation, the four pillars of our prosperity, are the most thriving when left most free to individual enterprise."

First Annual Message to Congress,
December 8, 1801
www.avalon.law.yale.edu/19th_century/Jeffmes1.asp

James Madison
Fourth President of the United States, 1809-1817

James Madison portrait by Gilbert Stuart, www.gilbert-stuart.org/JamesMadison

James Madison:

"A man has a property in his opinions and the free communication of them."

Essay in the National Gazette,
March 29, 1792
http://www.brainyquote.com/quotes/authors/j/james_madis
on

"As a man is said to have a right to his property, he may be equally said to have a property in his rights. Where an excess of power prevails, property of no sort is duly respected, no man is safe in his opinions, his person, his faculties, or his possessions."

Essay In the National Gazette Essay,

March 27, 1792
http://www.marksquotes.com/Founding-Fathers/JamesMadisonQuotes

"... If these rights are well defined, and secured against encroachment, it is impossible that government should ever degenerate into tyranny."

Speech to the 1st Congress introducing the Bill of Rights,
1789

http://books.google.com/books/"If these rights..."

"The diversity in the faculties of men, from which the rights of property originate, is not less an insuperable obstacle to a uniformity of interests.

The protection of these faculties is the first object of government."

The Independent Journal, Federalist #10,
November 22, 1787
http://www.brainyquote.com/quotes/authors/j/james_madison

"The rights of persons, and the rights of property, are the objects, for the protection of which Government was instituted."

Virginia Constitutional Convention,
December 2, 1829
http://www.brainyquote.com/quotes/authors/j/james_madison

"We may define a republic to be…a government which derives all its powers directly or indirectly from the great body of the people, and is administered by persons holding their offices during pleasure for a limited period, or during good behavior. It is essential to such a government that it be derived from the great body of the society, not from an inconsiderable proportion or a favored class of it…"

The Independent Journal, Federalist #39,
January 18, 1788
http://www.brainyquote.com/quotes/authors/j/james_madison

"The people are the only legitimate fountain of power, and it is from them that the constitutional charter, under which the several branches of government hold their power, is derived."

The Independent Journal, Federalist #49,
February 2, 1788
http://www.brainyquote.com/quotes/authors/j/james_madison

"The powers delegated by the proposed constitution to the federal government are few and defined. Those which are to remain in the State governments are numerous and indefinite...the powers reserved to the several States will extend to all the objects which, in the ordinary course of affairs, concern the lives, liberties and properties of the people, and the internal order, improvement and prosperity of the State."

The Independent Journal, Federalist #45,
January 26, 1788
http://www.marksquotes.com/Founding-Fathers/JamesMadisonQuotes

"The government of the United States is a definite government, confined to specified objects. It is not like state governments, whose powers are more general. Charity is no part of the legislative duty of the government"

Speech in the House of Representatives,
January 10, 1794
http://www.governmentquotes.mht/jamesmadison

"If Congress can do whatever in their discretion can be done by money, and will promote the General Welfare, the Government is no longer a limited one, possessing enumerated powers, but an indefinite one, subject to particular exceptions."

Letter to Edmund Pendleton, 1792
http://PatriotPost.us

"I believe there are more instances of the abridgement of freedom of the people by gradual and silent encroachments by those in power than by violent and sudden usurpations."

Virginia Convention on the ratification of the
Constitution, June 6, 1788
http://home.att.nt/~midflyer/madison

"An Elective Despotism was not the government we fought for, but one which should not only be founded on free principles, but in which the powers of government should be so divided and balanced among several bodies of magistracy, as that no one could transcend their legal limits, without being effectually checked and restrained by the others."

The Independent Journal, Federalist #48,
February 1, 1788
http://www.marksquotes.com/Founding-Fathers/JamesMadisonQuotes

"The class of citizens who provide at once their own food and their own raiment, may be viewed as the most truly independent and happy."

Essay in the National Gazette,
March 5, 1792
http://www.brainyquote.com/quotes/authors/j/james_madison

"…It is proper to take alarm at the first experiment upon our liberties."

Memorial to the Virginia
Legislature, 1785
http://books.google.com/books/"…It is proper"

"…a people who mean to be their own Governors, must arm themselves with the power which knowledge gives."

Letter to W. T. Barry,
August 4, 1822

http://www.marksquotes.com/Founding-Fathers/JamesMadisonQuotes

James Monroe
Fifth President of the United States, 1817-1825
James Monroe portrait by Gilbert Stuart, www.gilbert-stuart.org/JamesMonroe

James Monroe:

"The right of self defense never ceases. It is among the most sacred, and alike necessary, to nations and to individuals…"

Message to Congress,
November 16, 1818
http://www.brainyquote.com/quotes/authors/j/james_monroe

"To impose taxes when the public exigencies require them is an obligation of the most sacred character, especially with a free people."

State of the Union Address,
February 12, 1817
http://www.brainyquote.com/quotes/authors/j/james_monroe

"From the commencement of our Revolution to the present day almost forty years have elapsed, and from the establishment of this Constitution twenty-eight. Through this whole term the Government has been what may emphatically be called self-government. And what has been the effect? To whatever object we turn our attention, whether it relates to our foreign or domestic concerns, we find abundant cause to felicitate ourselves in the excellence of our institutions. During a period fraught with difficulties and marked by very extraordinary events the United States have flourished beyond example. Their citizens individually have been happy and the nation prosperous."

First Inaugural Address,
March 4, 1817
http://www.famousquotes.me.uk/speeches/presidential-speeches

"Under this Constitution our commerce has been wisely regulated with foreign nations and between the States; ... the States, respectively protected by the National Government under a mild, parental system against foreign dangers, and enjoying within their separate spheres, by a wise partition of power, a just proportion of the sovereignty, have improved their police, extended their settlements, and attained a strength and maturity which are the best proofs of wholesome laws well administered. And if we look to the condition of individuals what a proud spectacle does it exhibit! On whom has oppression fallen in any quarter of our Union? Who has been deprived of any right of person or property? Who restrained from offering his vows in the mode which he prefers to the Divine Author of his being? It is well known that all these blessings have been enjoyed in their fullest extent..."

First Inaugural Address,
March 4, 1817
http://www.famousquotes.me.uk/speeches/presidential-speeches

"They will choose competent and faithful representatives for every department. It is only when the people become ignorant and corrupt, when they degenerate into a populace, that they are incapable of exercising the sovereignty. Usurpation is then an easy attainment, and an usurper soon found. The people themselves become the willing instruments of their own debasement and ruin. Let us, then, look to the great cause, and endeavor to preserve it in full force. Let us by all wise and constitutional measures promote intelligence among the people as the best means of preserving our liberties.."

First Inaugural Address,
March 4, 1817
http://www.brainyquote.com/quotes/authors/j/james_madison

"…the highly favored condition of our country… is the interest of every citizen to maintain it. What are the dangers which menace us? If any exist they ought to be ascertained and guarded against."

First Inaugural Address,
March 4, 1817
http://www.famousquotes.me.uk/speeches/presidential-speeches

"National honor is national property of the highest value. The sentiment in the mind of every citizen is national strength. It ought therefore to be cherished."

First Inaugural Address,
March 4, 1817
http://www.brainyquote.com/quotes/authors/j/james_monroe

Author's Note:

The first five Presidents of the United States of America were among the Founding Fathers.

George Washington is called the Father of our Country.

Thomas Jefferson was the primary author of the Declaration of Independence.

James Madison is called the Father of the Constitution and was an author of the Bill of Rights and the Federalist Papers.

The Founding Principles of Liberty

1. The only reliable basis for sound government and just human relations is Natural Law.

2. A free people cannot survive under a republican constitution unless they remain virtuous and morally strong.

3. The most promising method of securing a virtuous and morally stable people is to elect virtuous leaders.

4. Without religion the government of a free people cannot be maintained.

5. All things were created by God, therefore upon Him all mankind are equally dependent, and to

Him they are equally responsible.

6. All men are created equal.

7. The proper role of government is to protect equal rights, not provide equal things.

8. Men are endowed by their Creator with certain unalienable rights.

9. To protect man's rights, God has revealed certain principles of divine law.

10. The God-given right to govern is vested in the sovereign authority of the whole people.

11. The majority of the people may alter or abolish a government which has become tyrannical.

12. The United States of America shall be a republic.

13. A constitution should be structured to permanently protect the people from the human frailties of their rulers.

14. Life and liberty are secure only so long as the right of property is secure.

15. The highest level of prosperity occurs when there is a free-market economy and a minimum of government regulations.

16. The government should be separated into three branches – legislative, executive, and judicial.

17. A system of checks and balances should be adopted to prevent the abuse of power.

18. The unalienable rights of the people are most likely to be preserved if the principles of government are set forth in a written constitution.

19. Only limited and carefully defined powers should be delegated to government, all others being retained in the people.

20. Efficiency and dispatch require government to operate according to the will of the majority, but constitutional provisions must be made to protect the rights of the minority.

21. Strong local self-government is the keystone to preserving human freedom.

22. A free people should be governed by law and not by the whims of men.

23. A free society cannot survive as a republic without a broad program of general education.

24. A free people will not survive unless they stay strong.

25. "Peace, commerce, and honest friendship

with all nations - entangling alliances with none." (Thomas Jefferson, 1st Inaugural Address, March 4, 1801)

26. The core unit which determines the strength of any society is the family; therefore, the government should foster and protect its integrity.

27. The burden of debt is as destructive to freedom as subjugation by conquest.

28. The United States has a manifest destiny to be an example and a blessing to the entire human race.

Source: "Over 150 volumes of the Founding Fathers original writings, minutes, letters, biographies, etc. distilled in The Five Thousand Year Leap, by Dr. W. Cleon Skousen, published by The National Center for Constitutional Studies, 1981." Founding principles necessary for liberty and freedom. Verbal permission to reprint, February 17, 2010. For more information, visit http://www.nccs.net.

The Pledge of Allegiance

I pledge allegiance to the Flag of the United States of America, and to the Republic for which it stands: one Nation under God, indivisible, with Liberty and Justice for all."

Francis Bellamy, August, 1892
http://www.ushistory.org/documents/pledge.htm

http://www.oldtimeislands.org/pledge/pledge/htm

Author's Note: Francis Bellamy is credited with the original version which reads: "I pledge allegiance to my Flag and the Republic for which it stands, one nation, indivisible, with liberty and justice for all." In 1924, the Pledge's words, 'my Flag' were changed to 'the Flag of the United States of America'. In 1954, the words 'under God' were added by Congress.

The Declaration of Independence

IN CONGRESS, July 4, 1776.

The unanimous Declaration of the thirteen united States of America,

WHEN in the course of human events, it becomes necessary for one people to dissolve the political bands which have connected them with another, and to assume among the powers of the earth, the separate and equal station to which the laws of nature and of nature's God entitle them, a decent respect to the opinions of mankind requires that they should declare the causes which impel them to the separation.

We hold these truths to be self-evident: That all men are created equal; that they are endowed by their Creator with certain unalienable rights; that among these are life, liberty, and the pursuit of happiness; that, to secure these rights, governments are instituted among men, deriving their just powers from the consent of the governed; that whenever any form of government becomes destructive of these ends, it is the right of the people to alter or to abolish it, and to institute new government, laying its foundation on such principles, and organizing its powers in such form, as to them shall seem most likely to effect their safety and happiness. Prudence, indeed, will dictate that governments long established should not be changed for light and transient causes; and accordingly all experience hath shown that mankind are more disposed to suffer, while evils are sufferable than to right themselves by abolishing the forms to which they are accustomed. But when a long train of abuses and usurpations, pursuing invariably the same object, evinces a design to reduce them under absolute despotism, it is their right, it is their duty, to throw off such government, and to provide new guards for their future security. Such has been the patient sufferance of these colonies; and such is now the necessity which constrains them to alter their former systems of government. The history of the present King of Great Britain is a history of repeated injuries and usurpations, all having in direct object the establishment of an absolute tyranny over these states. To prove this, let facts be submitted to a candid world.

He has refused his assent to laws, the most

wholesome and necessary for the public good.

He has forbidden his governors to pass laws of immediate and pressing importance, unless suspended in their operation till his assent should be obtained; and, when so suspended, he has utterly neglected to attend to them.

He has refused to pass other laws for the accommodation of large districts of people, unless those people would relinquish the right of representation in the legislature, a right inestimable to them, and formidable to tyrants only.

He has called together legislative bodies at places unusual uncomfortable, and distant from the depository of their public records, for the sole purpose of fatiguing them into compliance with his measures.

He has dissolved representative houses repeatedly, for opposing, with manly firmness, his invasions on the rights of the people.

He has refused for a long time, after such dissolutions, to cause others to be elected; whereby the legislative powers, incapable of annihilation, have returned to the people at large for their exercise; the state remaining, in the mean time, exposed to all the dangers of invasions from without and convulsions within.

He has endeavored to prevent the population of these states; for that purpose obstructing the laws for naturalization of foreigners; refusing to pass others to encourage their migration hither, and raising the conditions of new appropriations of lands.

He has obstructed the administration of justice, by refusing his assent to laws for establishing judiciary powers.

He has made judges dependent on his will alone, for the tenure of their offices, and the amount and payment of their salaries.

He has erected a multitude of new offices, and sent hither swarms of officers to harass our people and eat out their substance.

He has kept among us, in times of peace, standing armies, without the consent of our legislatures.

He has affected to render the military independent of, and superior to, the civil power.

He has combined with others to subject us to a jurisdiction foreign to our Constitution and unacknowledged by our laws, giving his assent to their acts of pretended legislation:

For quartering large bodies of armed troops among us;

For protecting them, by a mock trial, from punishment for any murders which they should commit on the inhabitants of these states;

For cutting off our trade with all parts of the world;

For imposing taxes on us without our consent;

For depriving us, in many cases, of the benefits of trial by jury;

For transporting us beyond seas, to be tried for pretended offenses;

For abolishing the free system of English laws in a neighboring province, establishing therein an arbitrary government, and enlarging its boundaries, so as to render it at once an example and fit instrument for introducing the same absolute rule into these colonies;

For taking away our charters, abolishing our most valuable laws, and altering fundamentally the forms of our governments;

For suspending our own legislatures, and declaring themselves invested with power to legislate for us in all cases whatsoever.

He has abdicated government here, by declaring us out of his protection and waging war against us.

He has plundered our seas, ravaged our coasts, burned our towns, and destroyed the lives of our people.

He is at this time transporting large armies of foreign mercenaries to complete the works of death, desolation, and tyranny already begun with circumstances of cruelty and perfidy scarcely paralleled in the most barbarous ages, and totally unworthy the head of a civilized nation.

He has constrained our fellow-citizens, taken captive on the high seas, to bear arms against their country, to become the executioners of their friends and brethren, or to fall themselves by their hands.

He has excited domestic insurrection among us, and has endeavored to bring on the inhabitants of our frontiers the merciless Indian savages, whose known rule of warfare is an undistinguished destruction of all ages, sexes, and conditions.

In every stage of these oppressions we have petitioned for redress in the most humble terms; our repeated petitions have been answered only by repeated injury. A prince, whose character is thus marked by every act which may define a tyrant, is unfit to be the ruler of a free people.

Nor have we been wanting in our attentions to our British brethren. We have warned them, from time to time, of attempts by their legislature to extend an unwarrantable jurisdiction over us. We have reminded them of the circumstances of our emigration and settlement here. We have appealed to their native justice and magnanimity; and we have conjured them, by the ties of our common kindred, to disavow these usurpations which would inevitably interrupt our connections and correspondence. They too, have been deaf to the voice of justice and of consanguinity. We must, therefore, acquiesce in the necessity which denounces our separation, and hold them as we hold the rest of mankind, enemies in war, in peace friends.

We, therefore, the representatives of the United

States of America, in General Congress assembled, appealing to the Supreme Judge of the world for the rectitude of our intentions, do, in the name and by the authority of the good people of these colonies solemnly publish and declare, That these United Colonies are, and of right ought to be, *FREE AND INDEPENDENT STATES;* that they are absolved from all allegiance to the British crown and that all political connection between them and the state of Great Britain is, and ought to be totally dissolved; and that, as free and independent states, they have full power to levy war, conclude peace, contract alliances, establish commerce, and do all other acts and things which independent states may of right do. And for the support of this declaration, with a firm reliance on the protection of Divine Providence, we mutually pledge to each other our lives, our fortunes, and our sacred honor.

Source: http://www.foundingfathers.info/foundingdocuments/DeclarationOfIndependence

Connecticut: Samuel Huntington, Roger Sherman, William Williams, Oliver Wolcott

Delaware: George Read, Thomas McKean, Caesar Rodney

Georgia: Button Gwinett, Lyman Hall, George Walton

Maryland: Charles Carroll, Samuel Chase, Thomas Stone, William Paca

Massachusetts: John Adams, Samuel Adams, John Hancock, Robert Treat Paine, Elbridge Gerry

New Hampshire: Josiah Bartlett, William Whipple, Matthew Thornton

New Jersey: Abraham Clark, John Hart, Francis Hopkinson, Richard Stockton, John Witherspoon

New York: Lewis Morris, Francis Lewis, Philip Livingston, William Floyd

North Carolina: William Hooper, John Penn, Joseph Hewes

Pennsylvania: George Clymer, Robert Morris, Benjamin Franklin, John Morton, Benjamin Rush, George Ross, James Smith, James Wilson, George Taylor

Rhode Island: Stephen Hopkins, William Ellery

South Carolina: Edward Rutledge, Arthur Middleton, Thomas Lynch, Jr., Thomas Heyward, Jr.

Virginia: Richard Henry Lee, Francis Lightfoot Lee, Carter Braxton, Benjamin Harrison, Thomas Jefferson, George Wythe, Thomas Nelson, Jr.

The Constitution of the United States of America

We the People of the United States, in Order to form a more perfect Union, establish Justice, insure domestic Tranquility, provide for the common defense, promote the general Welfare, and secure the Blessings of Liberty to ourselves and our Posterity, do ordain and establish this Constitution for the United States of America.

Article I

Section 1
All legislative Powers herein granted shall be vested in a Congress of the United States, which shall consist of a Senate and House of Representatives.

Section 2
The House of Representatives shall be composed of Members chosen every second Year by the People of the several States, and the Electors in each State shall have the Qualifications requisite for Electors of the most numerous Branch of the State Legislature. No Person shall be a Representative

who shall not have attained to the Age of twenty five Years, and been seven Years a Citizen of the United States, and who shall not, when elected, be an Inhabitant of that State in which he shall be chosen.

Representatives and direct Taxes shall be apportioned among the several States which may be included within this Union, according to their respective Numbers, which shall be determined by adding to the whole Number of free Persons, including those bound to Service for a Term of Years, and excluding Indians not taxed, three fifths of all other Persons. The actual Enumeration shall be made within three Years after the first Meeting of the Congress of the United States, and within every subsequent Term of ten Years, in such Manner as they shall by Law direct. The Number of Representatives shall not exceed one for every thirty Thousand, but each State shall have at Least one Representative; and until such enumeration shall be made, the State of New Hampshire shall be entitled to choose three, Massachusetts eight, Rhode-Island and Providence Plantations one, Connecticut five, New York six, New Jersey four, Pennsylvania eight, Delaware one, Maryland six, Virginia ten, North Carolina five, South Carolina five, and Georgia three.

When vacancies happen in the Representation from

any State, the Executive Authority thereof shall issue Writs of Election to fill such Vacancies.

The House of Representatives shall choose their Speaker and other Officers; and shall have the sole Power of Impeachment.

Section 3
The Senate of the United States shall be composed of two Senators from each State, chosen by the Legislature thereof for six Years; and each Senator shall have one Vote.

Immediately after they shall be assembled in Consequence of the first Election, they shall be divided as equally as may be into three Classes. The Seats of the Senators of the first Class shall be vacated at the Expiration of the second Year, of the second Class at the Expiration of the fourth Year, and of the third Class at the Expiration of the sixth Year, so that one third may be chosen every second Year; and if Vacancies happen by Resignation, or otherwise, during the Recess of the Legislature of any State, the Executive thereof may make temporary Appointments until the next Meeting of the Legislature, which shall then fill such Vacancies.

No Person shall be a Senator who shall not have attained to the Age of thirty Years, and been nine Years a Citizen of the United States, and who shall not, when elected, be an Inhabitant of that State for which he shall be chosen.

The Vice President of the United States shall be President of the Senate, but shall have no Vote, unless they be equally divided.

The Senate shall choose their other Officers, and also a President pro tempore, in the Absence of the Vice President, or when he shall exercise the Office of President of the United States.

The Senate shall have the sole Power to try all Impeachments. When sitting for that Purpose, they shall be on Oath or Affirmation. When the President of the United States is tried, the Chief Justice shall preside; And no person shall be convicted without the Concurrence of two thirds of the Members present. Judgment in Cases of Impeachment shall not extend further than to removal from Office, and disqualification to hold and enjoy any Office of honor, Trust or Profit under the United States: but the Party convicted shall nevertheless be liable and subject to Indictment, Trial, Judgment and Punishment, according to Law.

Section 4
The Times, Places and Manner of holding Elections for Senators and Representatives, shall be prescribed in each State by the Legislature thereof; but the Congress may at any time by Law make or

alter such Regulations, except as to the Places of choosing Senators.

The Congress shall assemble at least once in every Year, and such Meeting shall be on the first Monday in December, unless they shall by Law appoint a different Day.

Section 5
Each House shall be the Judge of the Elections, Returns and Qualifications of its own Members, and a Majority of each shall constitute a Quorum to do Business; but a smaller Number may adjourn from day to day, and may be authorized to compel the Attendance of absent Members, in such Manner, and under such Penalties as each House may provide.

Each House may determine the Rules of its Proceedings, punish its Members for disorderly Behavior, and, with the Concurrence of two thirds, expel a Member.

Each House shall keep a Journal of its Proceedings, and from time to time publish the same, excepting such Parts as may in their Judgment require Secrecy; and the Yeas and Nays of the Members of either House on any question shall, at the Desire of one fifth of those Present, be entered on the Journal.

Neither House, during the Session of Congress,

shall, without the Consent of the other, adjourn for more than three days, nor to any other Place than that in which the two Houses shall be sitting.

Section 6
The Senators and Representatives shall receive a Compensation for their Services, to be ascertained by Law, and paid out of the Treasury of the United States. They shall in all Cases, except Treason, Felony and Breach of the Peace, be privileged from Arrest during their Attendance at the Session of their respective Houses, and in going to and returning from the same; and for any Speech or Debate in either House, they shall not be questioned in any other Place.

No Senator or Representative shall, during the Time for which he was elected, be appointed to any civil Office under the Authority of the United States, which shall have been created, or the Emoluments whereof shall have been increased during such time; and no Person holding any Office under the United States, shall be a Member of either House during his Continuance in Office.

Section 7
All Bills for raising Revenue shall originate in the House of Representatives; but the Senate may propose or concur with Amendments as on other Bills.   Every Bill which shall have passed the House of Representatives and the Senate, shall,

before it become a Law, be presented to the President of the United States: If he approve he shall sign it, but if not he shall return it, with his Objections to that House in which it shall have originated, who shall enter the Objections at large on their Journal, and proceed to reconsider it.

If after such Reconsideration two thirds of that House shall agree to pass the Bill, it shall be sent, together with the Objections, to the other House, by which it shall likewise be reconsidered, and if approved by two thirds of that House, it shall become a Law. But in all such Cases the Votes of both Houses shall be determined by Yeas and Nays, and the Names of the Persons voting for and against the Bill shall be entered on the Journal of each House respectively.

If any Bill shall not be returned by the President within ten Days (Sundays excepted) after it shall have been presented to him, the Same shall be a Law, in like Manner as if he had signed it, unless the Congress by their Adjournment prevent its Return, in which Case it shall not be a Law.

Every Order, Resolution, or Vote to which the Concurrence of the Senate and House of Representatives may be necessary (except on a question of Adjournment) shall be presented to the President of the United States; and before the Same shall take Effect, shall be approved by him, or being disapproved by him, shall be repassed by two thirds of the Senate and House of Representatives, according to the Rules and Limitations prescribed in the Case of a Bill.

Section 8
The Congress shall have Power To lay and collect Taxes, Duties, Imposts and Excises, to pay the Debts and provide for the common Defense and general Welfare of the United States; but all Duties, Imposts and Excises shall be uniform throughout the United States;

To borrow Money on the credit of the United States;

To regulate Commerce with foreign Nations, and among the several States, and with the Indian Tribes;

To establish an uniform Rule of Naturalization, and uniform Laws on the subject of Bankruptcies throughout the United States;

To coin Money, regulate the Value thereof, and of foreign Coin, and fix the Standard of Weights and Measures;

To provide for the Punishment of counterfeiting the Securities and current Coin of the United States;

To establish Post Offices and post Roads;

To promote the Progress of Science and useful Arts, by securing for limited Times to Authors and Inventors the exclusive Right to their respective Writings and Discoveries;

To constitute Tribunals inferior to the supreme Court;

To define and punish Piracies and Felonies Committed on the high seas, and Offenses against the Law of Nations;

To declare War, grant Letters of Marque and Reprisal, and make Rules concerning Captures on Land and Water;

To raise and support Armies, but no Appropriation of Money to that Use shall be for a longer Term than two Years;

To provide and maintain a Navy;

To make Rules for the Government and Regulation of the land and naval Forces;

To provide for calling forth the Militia to execute the Laws of the Union, suppress Insurrections and repel Invasions;

To provide for organizing, arming, and disciplining, the Militia, and for governing such Part of them as may be employed in the Service of the United States, reserving to the States respectively, the Appointment of the Officers, and the Authority of training the Militia according to the discipline prescribed by Congress;

To exercise exclusive Legislation in all Cases what-so-ever, over such District (not exceeding ten Miles square) as may, by Cession of particular States, and the Acceptance of Congress, become the Seat of the Government of the United States, and to exercise like Authority over all Places purchased by the Consent of the Legislature of the State in which the Same shall be, for the Erection of Forts, Magazines, Arsenals, dockyards, and other needful Buildings;--And

To make all Laws which shall be necessary and proper for carrying into Execution the foregoing Powers, and all other Powers vested by this
The Migration or Importation of such Persons as any of the States now existing shall think proper to admit, shall not be prohibited by the Congress prior to the Year one thousand eight hundred and eight, but a Tax or duty may be imposed on such Importation, not exceeding ten dollars for each Person.

Section 9
The Migration or Importation of such Persons

as any of the States now existing shall think proper to admit, shall not be prohibited by the Congress prior to the Year one thousand eight hundred and eight, but a Tax or duty may be imposed on such Importation, not exceeding ten dollars for each Person.

The Privilege of the Writ of Habeas Corpus shall not be suspended, unless when in Cases of Rebellion or Invasion the public Safety may require it.

No Bill of Attainder or ex post facto Law shall be passed.

No Capitation, or other direct, Tax shall be laid, unless in Proportion to the Census or enumeration herein before directed to be taken.

No Tax or Duty shall be laid on Articles exported from any State.

No Preference shall be given by any Regulation of Commerce or Revenue to the Ports of one State over those of another; nor shall Vessels bound to, or from, one State, be obliged to enter, clear, or pay Duties in another.

No Money shall be drawn from the Treasury, but in Consequence of Appropriations made by Law; and a regular Statement and Account of the

Receipts and Expenditures of all public Money shall be published from time to time.

No Title of Nobility shall be granted by the United States: And no Person holding any Office of Profit or Trust under them, shall, without the Consent of the Congress, accept of any present, Emolument, Office, or Title, of any kind whatever, from any King, Prince, or foreign State.

Section 10

No State shall enter into any Treaty, Alliance, or Confederation; grant Letters of Marque and Reprisal; coin Money; emit Bills of Credit; make any Thing but gold and silver Coin a Tender in Payment of Debts; pass any Bill of Attainder, ex post facto Law, or Law impairing the Obligation of Contracts, or grant any Title of Nobility.

No State shall, without the Consent of the Congress, lay any Imposts or Duties on Imports or Exports, except what may be absolutely necessary for executing it's inspection Laws: and the net Produce of all Duties and Imposts, laid by any State on Imports or Exports, shall be for the Use of the Treasury of the United States; and all such Laws shall be subject to the Revision and Control of the Congress.

No State shall, without the Consent of Congress, lay any Duty of Tonnage, keep Troops, or Ships of War in time of Peace, enter into any Agreement or Compact with another State, or with a foreign Power, or engage in War, unless actually invaded, or in such imminent Danger as will not admit of delay.

Article II

Section 1
The executive Power shall be vested in a President of the United States of America. He shall hold his Office during the Term of four Years, and, together with the Vice President, chosen for the same Term, be elected, as follows:

Each State shall appoint, in such Manner as the Legislature thereof may direct, a Number of Electors, equal to the whole Number of Senators and Representatives to which the State may be entitled in the Congress: but no Senator or Representative, or Person holding an Office of Trust or Profit under the United States, shall be appointed an Elector.

The Electors shall meet in their respective States, and vote by Ballot for two Persons, of whom one at least shall not be an Inhabitant of the same State with themselves. And they shall make a List of all the Persons voted for, and of the Number of Votes for each; which List they shall sign and certify, and transmit sealed to the Seat of the Government of the

United States, directed to the President of the Senate.

The President of the Senate shall, in the Presence of the Senate and House of Representatives, open all the Certificates, and the Votes shall then be counted. The Person having the greatest Number of Votes shall be the President, if such Number be a Majority of the whole Number of Electors appointed; and if there be more than one who have such Majority, and have an equal Number of Votes, then the House of Representatives shall immediately choose by Ballot one of them for President; and if no Person have a Majority, then from the five highest on the List the said House shall in like Manner choose the President. But in choosing the President, the Votes shall be taken by States, the Representation from each State having one Vote; A quorum for this purpose shall consist of a Member or Members from two thirds of the States, and a Majority of all the States shall be necessary to a Choice.

In every Case, after the Choice of the President, the Person having the greatest Number of Votes of the Electors shall be the Vice President. But if there should remain two or more who have equal Votes, the Senate shall choose from them by Ballot the Vice President.

The Congress may determine the Time of choosing

the Electors, and the Day on which they shall give their Votes; which Day shall be the same throughout the United States.

No Person except a natural born Citizen, or a Citizen of the United States, at the time of the Adoption of this Constitution, shall be eligible to the Office of President; neither shall any Person be eligible to that Office who shall not have attained to the Age of thirty five Years, and been fourteen Years a Resident within the United States.

In Case of the Removal of the President from Office, or of his Death, Resignation, or Inability to discharge the Powers and Duties of the said Office, the Same shall devolve on the Vice President, and the Congress may by Law provide for the Case of Removal, Death, Resignation or Inability, both of the President and Vice President, declaring what Officer shall then act as President, and such Officer shall act accordingly, until the Disability be removed, or a President shall be elected.

The President shall, at stated Times, receive for his Services, a Compensation, which shall neither be increased nor diminished during the Period for which he shall have been elected, and he shall not receive within that Period any other Emolument from the United States, or any of them.

Before he enter on the Execution of his Office, he

shall take the following Oath or Affirmation:
"I do solemnly swear (or affirm) that I will
faithfully execute the Office of President of the
United States, and will to the best of my Ability,
preserve, protect and defend the Constitution of the
United States."

Section 2
The President shall be Commander in Chief of the
Army and Navy of the United States, and of the
Militia of the several States, when called into the
actual Service of the United States; he may require
the Opinion, in writing, of the principal Officer in
each of the executive Departments, upon any Subject relating to the Duties of their respective
Offices, and he shall have Power to grant Reprieves
and Pardons for Offences against the United States,
except in Cases of Impeachment.

He shall have Power, by and with the Advice and
Consent of the Senate, to make Treaties, provided
two thirds of the Senators present concur; and he
shall nominate, and by and with the Advice and
Consent of the Senate, shall appoint Ambassadors,
 her public Ministers and Consuls, Judges of the
supreme Court, and all other Officers of the United
States, whose Appointments are not herein
otherwise provided for, and which shall be
established by Law: but the Congress may by Law
vest the Appointment of such inferior Officers, as
they think proper, in the President alone, in the

Courts of Law, or in the Heads of Departments.

The President shall have Power to fill up all Vacancies that may happen during the Recess of the Senate, by granting Commissions which shall expire at the End of their next Session.

Section 3
He shall from time to time give to the Congress Information of the State of the Union, and recommend to their Consideration such Measures as he shall judge necessary and expedient; he may, on extraordinary Occasions, convene both Houses, or either of them, and in Case of Disagreement between them, with Respect to the Time of Adjournment, he may adjourn them to such Time as he shall think proper; he shall receive Ambassadors and other public Ministers; he shall take Care that the Laws be faithfully executed, and shall Commission all the Officers of the United States.

Section 4
The President, Vice President and all civil Officers of the United States, shall be removed from Office on Impeachment for, and Conviction of, Treason, Bribery, or other high Crimes and Misdemeanors.

Article III

Section 1
The Judicial Power of the United States shall be

vested in one supreme Court, and in such inferior Courts as the Congress may from time to time ordain and establish. The Judges, both of the supreme and inferior Courts, shall hold their Offices during good Behavior, and shall, at stated Times, receive for their Services a Compensation, which shall not be diminished during their Continuance in Office.

Section 2
The judicial Power shall extend to all Cases, in Law and Equity, arising under this Constitution, the Laws of the United States, and Treaties made, or which shall be made, under their Authority;--to all Cases affecting Ambassadors, other public Ministers and Consuls;--to all Cases of admiralty and maritime Jurisdiction;--to Controversies to which the United States shall be a Party;--to Controversies between two or more States;-- between a State and Citizens of another State;-- between Citizens of different States;--between Citizens of the same State claiming Lands under Grants of different States, and between a State, or the Citizens thereof, and foreign States, Citizens or Subjects.

In all Cases affecting Ambassadors, other public Ministers and Consuls, and those in which a State shall be Party, the Supreme Court shall have original Jurisdiction. In all the other Cases before mentioned, the Supreme Court shall have appellate

Jurisdiction, both as to Law and Fact, with such Exceptions, and under such Regulations as the Congress shall make.

The Trial of all Crimes, except in Cases of Impeachment, shall be by Jury; and such Trial shall be held in the State where the said Crimes shall have been committed; but when not committed within any State, the Trial shall be at such Place or Places as the Congress may by Law have directed.

Section 3
Treason against the United States, shall consist only in levying War against them, or in adhering to their Enemies, giving them Aid and Comfort. No Person shall be convicted of Treason unless on the Testimony of two Witnesses to the same overt Act, or on Confession in open Court.

The Congress shall have Power to declare the Punishment of Treason, but no Attainder of Treason shall work Corruption of Blood, or Forfeiture except during the Life of the Person attainted.

Article IV

Section 1
Full Faith and Credit shall be given in each State to the public Acts, Records, and judicial Proceedings of every other State. And the Congress may by general Laws prescribe the Manner in which such

Acts, Records and Proceedings shall be proved, and the effect thereof.

Section 2

The Citizens of each State shall be entitled to all Privileges and Immunities of Citizens in the several States.

A Person charged in any State with Treason, Felony, or other Crime, who shall flee from Justice, and be found in another State, shall on Demand of the executive Authority of the State from which he fled, be delivered up, to be removed to the State having Jurisdiction of the Crime.

No Person held to Service or Labor in one State, under the Laws thereof, escaping into another, shall, in Consequence of any Law or Regulation therein, be discharged from such Service or Labor, but shall be delivered up on Claim of the Party to whom such Service or Labor may be due.

Section 3

New States may be admitted by the Congress into this Union; but no new State shall be formed or erected within the Jurisdiction of any other State; nor any State be formed by the Junction of two or more States, or Parts of States, without the Consent of the Legislatures of the States concerned as well as of the Congress.

The Congress shall have Power to dispose of and make all needful Rules and Regulations respecting the Territory or other Property belonging to the United States; and nothing in this Constitution shall be so construed as to Prejudice any Claims of the United States, or of any particular State.

Section 4
The United States shall guarantee to every State in this Union a Republican Form of Government, and shall protect each of them against Invasion; and on Application of the Legislature, or of the Executive (when the Legislature cannot be convened), against domestic Violence.

Article V
The Congress, whenever two thirds of both Houses shall deem it necessary, shall propose Amendments to this Constitution, or, on the Application of the Legislatures of two thirds of the several States, shall call a Convention for proposing Amendments, which, in either Case, shall be valid to all Intents and Purposes, as Part of this Constitution, when ratified by the Legislatures of three fourths of the several States, or by Conventions in three fourths thereof, as the one or the other Mode of Ratification may be proposed by the Congress; Provided that no Amendment which may be made prior to the Year One thousand eight hundred and eight shall in any Manner affect the first and fourth Clauses in the Ninth Section of the first Article; and that no State,

without its Consent, shall be deprived of its equal Suffrage in the Senate.

Article VI

All Debts contracted and Engagements entered into, before the Adoption of this Constitution, shall be as valid against the United States under this Constitution, as under the Confederation.

This Constitution, and the Laws of the United States which shall be made in Pursuance thereof; and all Treaties made, or which shall be made, under the Authority of the United States, shall be the supreme Law of the Land; and the Judges in every State shall be bound thereby, any Thing in the Constitution or Laws of any State to the Contrary notwithstanding.

The Senators and Representatives before mentioned, and the Members of the several State Legislatures, and all executive and judicial Officers, both of the United States and of the several States, shall be bound by Oath or Affirmation, to support this Constitution; but no religious Test shall ever be required as a Qualification to any Office or public Trust under the United States.

Article VII

The Ratification of the Conventions of nine States, shall be sufficient for the Establishment of this

Constitution between the States so ratifying the Same.

Done in Convention by the Unanimous Consent of the States present the Seventeenth Day of September in the Year of our Lord one thousand seven hundred and Eighty seven and of the Independence of the United States of America the Twelfth In witness whereof We have hereunto subscribed our Names,...

Source: http://www.foundingfathers.info/foundingdocuments/TheU.S.Constitution

Connecticut: William Samuel Johnson, Roger Sherman
Delaware: Richard Bassett, Gunning Bedford, Jr., Jacob Broom, John Dickinson, George Read
Georgia: Abraham Baldwin, William Few, Jr.
Maryland: Daniel Carroll, Daniel Jenifer, James McIlenry
Massachusetts: Nathaniel Gorham, Rufus King
New Hampshire: Nicholas Gilman, John Langdon
New Jersey: David Brearly, Jonathon Dayton, William Livingston, William Paterson
New York: Alexander Hamilton
North Carolina: William Blount, Richard Dobbs Spaight, Hugh Williamson
Pennsylvania: George Clymer, Thomas Fitzsimmons, Benjamin Franklin, Jared Ingersoll, Thomas Mifflin, Gouvernor Morris, Robert Morris, James Wilson
Rhode Island: Stephen Hopkins, William Ellery
South Carolina: Pierce Butler, Charles Pinckney, Charles Cotesworth Pinckney, John Rutledge
Virginia: John Blair, James Madison, George Washington

The Bill of Rights

The Preamble to The Bill of Rights

Congress of the United States begun and held at the City of New-York, on Wednesday the fourth of March, one thousand seven hundred and eighty nine.

THE Conventions of a number of the States, having at the time of their adopting the Constitution, expressed a desire, in order to prevent misconstruction or abuse of its powers, that further declaratory and restrictive clauses should be added: And as extending the ground of public confidence in the Government, will best ensure the beneficent ends of its institution.

RESOLVED by the Senate and House of Representatives of the United States of America, in Congress assembled, two thirds of both Houses concurring, that the following Articles be proposed to the Legislatures of the several States, as amendments to the Constitution of the United States, all, or any of which Articles, when ratified by three fourths of the said Legislatures, to be valid to all intents and purposes, as part of the said Constitution; viz.

ARTICLES in addition to, and Amendment of the Constitution of the United States of America, proposed by Congress, and ratified by the Legislatures of the several States, pursuant to the fifth Article of the original Constitution.

Note: The following text is a transcription of the first ten amendments to the Constitution in their original form. These amendments were ratified December 15, 1791, and form what is known as the "Bill of Rights."

Amendment I

Congress shall make no law respecting an establishment of religion, or prohibiting the free exercise thereof; or abridging the freedom of speech, or of the press; or the right of the people peaceably to assemble, and to petition the Government for a redress of grievances.

Amendment II

A well regulated Militia, being necessary to the security of a free State, the right of the people to keep and bear Arms, shall not be infringed.

Amendment III

No Soldier shall, in time of peace be quartered in any house, without the consent of the Owner, nor in time of war, but in a manner to be prescribed by law.

Amendment IV

The right of the people to be secure in their persons, houses, papers, and effects, against unreasonable searches and seizures, shall not be violated, and no Warrants shall issue, but upon probable cause, supported by Oath or affirmation, and particularly describing the place to be searched, and the persons or things to be seized.

Amendment V

No person shall be held to answer for a capital, or otherwise infamous crime, unless on a presentment or indictment of a Grand Jury, except in cases arising in the land or naval forces, or in the Militia, when in actual service in time of War or public danger; nor shall any person be subject for the same offence to be twice put in jeopardy of life or limb; nor shall be compelled in any criminal case to be a witness against himself, nor be deprived of life, liberty, or property, without due process of law; nor shall private property be taken for public use, without just compensation.

Amendment VI

In all criminal prosecutions, the accused shall enjoy the right to a speedy and public trial, by an impartial jury of the State and district wherein the crime shall have been committed, which district shall have been previously ascertained by law, and to be informed of the nature and cause of the accusation; to be confronted with the witnesses against him; to have compulsory process for obtaining witnesses in his favor, and to have the Assistance of Counsel for his defense.

Amendment VII

In Suits at common law, where the value in controversy shall exceed twenty dollars, the right of trial by jury shall be preserved, and no fact tried by a jury, shall be otherwise re-examined in any Court of the United States, than according to the rules of the common law.

Amendment VIII

Excessive bail shall not be required, nor excessive fines imposed, nor cruel and unusual punishments inflicted.

Amendment IX

The enumeration in the Constitution, of certain rights, shall not be construed to deny or disparage others retained by the people.

Amendment X

The powers not delegated to the United States by the Constitution, nor prohibited by it to the States, are reserved to the States respectively, or to the people.

Amendment XI

Passed by Congress March 4, 1794. Ratified February 7, 1795.

Note: Article III, section 2, of the Constitution was modified by amendment 11.

The Judicial power of the United States shall not be construed to extend to any suit in law or equity, commenced or prosecuted against one of the United

States by Citizens of another State, or by Citizens or Subjects of any Foreign State.

Amendment XII
Passed by Congress December 9, 1803. Ratified June 15, 1804.

Note: A portion of Article II, section 1 of the Constitution was superseded by the 12th amendment.

The Electors shall meet in their respective states and vote by ballot for President and Vice-President, one of whom, at least, shall not be an inhabitant of the same state with themselves; they shall name in their ballots the person voted for as President, and in distinct ballots the person voted for as Vice-President, and they shall make distinct lists of all persons voted for as President, and of all persons voted for as Vice-President, and of the number of votes for each, which lists they shall sign and certify, and transmit sealed to the seat of the government of the United States, directed to the President of the Senate; --

The President of the Senate shall, in the presence of the Senate and House of Representatives, open all the certificates and the votes shall then be counted; -

The person having the greatest number of votes for President, shall be the President, if such number be a majority of the whole number of Electors appointed; and if no person have such majority, then from the persons having the highest numbers not exceeding three on the list of those voted for as President, the House of Representatives shall choose immediately, by ballot, the President. But in choosing the President, the votes shall be taken by states, the representation from each state having one vote; a quorum for this purpose shall consist of a member or members from two-thirds of the states, and a majority of all the states shall be necessary to a choice. [And if the House of Representatives shall not choose a President whenever the right of choice shall devolve upon them, before the fourth day of March next following, then the Vice-President shall act as President, as in case of the death or other constitutional disability of the President. --]* The person having the greatest number of votes as Vice-President, shall be the Vice-President, if such number be a majority of the whole number of Electors appointed, and if no person have a majority, then from the two highest numbers on the list, the Senate shall choose the Vice-President; a quorum for the purpose shall consist of two-thirds of the whole number of Senators, and a majority of the whole number shall be necessary to a choice. But no person constitutionally ineligible to the office of President shall be eligible to that of Vice-President of the United States.

*Superseded by section 3 of the 20th amendment.

Amendment XIII

Passed by Congress January 31, 1865. Ratified December 6, 1865.

Note: A portion of Article IV, section 2, of the Constitution was superseded by the 13th amendment.

Section 1.

Neither slavery nor involuntary servitude, except as a punishment for crime whereof the party shall have been duly convicted, shall exist within the United States, or any place subject to their jurisdiction.

Section 2.

Congress shall have power to enforce this article by appropriate legislation.

Amendment XIV

Passed by Congress June 13, 1866. Ratified July 9, 1868.

Note: Article I, section 2, of the Constitution was modified by section 2 of the 14th amendment.

Section 1.

All persons born or naturalized in the United States, and subject to the jurisdiction thereof, are citizens of the United States and of the State wherein they reside. No State shall make or enforce any law which shall abridge the privileges or immunities of citizens of the United States; nor shall any State deprive any person of life, liberty, or property, without due process of law; nor deny to any person within its jurisdiction the equal protection of the laws.

Section 2.

Representatives shall be apportioned among the several States according to their respective numbers, counting the whole number of persons in each State, excluding Indians not taxed. But when the right to vote at any election for the choice of electors for President and Vice-President of the United States, Representatives in Congress, the Executive and Judicial officers of a State, or the members of the Legislature thereof, is denied to any of the male inhabitants of such State, being twenty-one years of age,* and citizens of the United States, or in any way abridged, except for participation in rebellion, or other crime, the basis of representation therein shall be reduced in the proportion which the number of such male citizens shall bear to the whole number of male citizens twenty-one years of age in such State.

Section 3.

No person shall be a Senator or Representative in Congress, or elector of President and Vice-

President, or hold any office, civil or military, under the United States, or under any State, who, having previously taken an oath, as a member of Congress, or as an officer of the United States, or as a member of any State legislature, or as an executive or judicial officer of any State, to support the Constitution of the United States, shall have engaged in insurrection or rebellion against the same, or given aid or comfort to the enemies thereof. But Congress may by a vote of two-thirds of each House, remove such disability.

Section 4.

The validity of the public debt of the United States, authorized by law, including debts incurred for payment of pensions and bounties for services in suppressing insurrection or rebellion, shall not be questioned. But neither the United States nor any State shall assume or pay any debt or obligation incurred in aid of insurrection or rebellion against the United States, or any claim for the loss or emancipation of any slave; but all such debts, obligations and claims shall be held illegal and void.

Section 5.

The Congress shall have the power to enforce, by appropriate legislation, the provisions of this article.

Changed by section 1 of the 26th amendment.

Amendment XV

Passed by Congress February 26, 1869. Ratified February 3, 1870.

Section 1.

The right of citizens of the United States to vote shall not be denied or abridged by the United States or by any State on account of race, color, or previous condition of servitude--

Section 2.

The Congress shall have the power to enforce this article by appropriate legislation.

Amendment XVI

Passed by Congress July 2, 1909. Ratified February 3, 1913.

Note: Article I, section 9, of the Constitution was modified by amendment 16.

The Congress shall have power to lay and collect taxes on incomes, from whatever source derived, without apportionment among the several States, and without regard to any census or enumeration.

Amendment XVII
Passed by Congress May 13, 1912. Ratified April 8, 1913.

Note: Article I, section 3, of the Constitution was modified by the 17th amendment.

The Senate of the United States shall be composed of two Senators from each State, elected by the people thereof, for six years; and each Senator shall have one vote. The electors in each State shall have the qualifications requisite for electors of the most numerous branch of the State legislatures.

When vacancies happen in the representation of any State in the Senate, the executive authority of such State shall issue writs of election to fill such vacancies: *Provided*, That the legislature of any State may empower the executive thereof to make temporary appointments until the people fill the vacancies by election as the legislature may direct.

This amendment shall not be so construed as to affect the election or term of any Senator chosen before it becomes valid as part of the Constitution.

Amendment XVIII
Passed by Congress December 18, 1917. Ratified January 16, 1919. Repealed by amendment 21.

Section 1.

After one year from the ratification of this article the manufacture, sale, or transportation of intoxicating liquors within, the importation thereof into, or the exportation thereof from the United States and all territory subject to the jurisdiction thereof for beverage purposes is hereby prohibited.

Section 2.

The Congress and the several States shall have concurrent power to enforce this article by appropriate legislation.

Section 3.

This article shall be inoperative unless it shall have been ratified as an amendment to the Constitution by the legislatures of the several States, as provided in the Constitution, within seven years from the date of the submission hereof to the States by the Congress.

Amendment XIX
Passed by Congress June 4, 1919. Ratified August 18, 1920.

The right of citizens of the United States to vote shall not be denied or abridged by the United States or by any State on account of sex.

Congress shall have power to enforce this article by appropriate legislation.

Amendment XX
Passed by Congress March 2, 1932. Ratified January 23, 1933.

Note: Article I, section 4, of the Constitution was modified by section 2 of this amendment. In addition, a portion of the 12th amendment was superseded by section 3.

Section 1.

The terms of the President and the Vice President shall end at noon on the 20th day of January, and the terms of Senators and Representatives at noon on the 3d day of January, of the years in which such terms would have ended if this article had not been ratified; and the terms of their successors shall then begin.

Section 2.

The Congress shall assemble at least once in every year, and such meeting shall begin at noon on the 3d day of January, unless they shall by law appoint a different day.

Section 3.

If, at the time fixed for the beginning of the term of the President, the President elect shall have died, the Vice President elect shall become President. If a President shall not have been chosen before the time fixed for the beginning of his term, or if the President elect shall have failed to qualify, then the

Vice President elect shall act as President until a President shall have qualified; and the Congress may by law provide for the case wherein neither a President elect nor a Vice President shall have qualified, declaring who shall then act as President, or the manner in which one who is to act shall be selected, and such person shall act accordingly until a President or Vice President shall have qualified.

Section 4.

The Congress may by law provide for the case of the death of any of the persons from whom the House of Representatives may choose a President whenever the right of choice shall have devolved upon them, and for the case of the death of any of the persons from whom the Senate may choose a Vice President whenever the right of choice shall have devolved upon them.

Section 5.

Sections 1 and 2 shall take effect on the 15th day of October following the ratification of this article.

Section 6.

This article shall be inoperative unless it shall have been ratified as an amendment to the Constitution by the legislatures of three-fourths of the several States within seven years from the date of its submission.

Amendment XXI

Passed by Congress February 20, 1933. Ratified December 5, 1933.

Section 1.

The eighteenth article of amendment to the Constitution of the United States is hereby repealed.

Section 2.

The transportation or importation into any State, Territory, or Possession of the United States for delivery or use therein of intoxicating liquors, in violation of the laws thereof, is hereby prohibited.

Section 3.

This article shall be inoperative unless it shall have been ratified as an amendment to the Constitution by conventions in the several States, as provided in the Constitution, within seven years from the date of the submission hereof to the States by the Congress.

Amendment XXII

Passed by Congress March 21, 1947. Ratified February 27, 1951.

Section 1.

No person shall be elected to the office of the President more than twice, and no person who has held the office of President, or acted as President, for more than two years of a term to which some other person was elected President shall be elected to the office of President more than once. But this Article shall not apply to any person holding the office of President when this Article was proposed by Congress, and shall not prevent any person who may be holding the office of President, or acting as President, during the term within which this Article becomes operative from holding the office of President or acting as President during the remainder of such term.

Section 2.

This article shall be inoperative unless it shall have been ratified as an amendment to the Constitution by the legislatures of three-fourths of the several States within seven years from the date of its submission to the States by the Congress.

Amendment XXIII
Passed by Congress June 16, 1960. Ratified March 29, 1961.

Section 1.

The District constituting the seat of Government of the United States shall appoint in such manner as Congress may direct: A number of electors of President and Vice President equal to the whole number of Senators and Representatives in Congress to which the District would be entitled if it were a State, but in no event more than the least populous State; they shall be in addition to those appointed by the States, but they shall be considered, for the purposes of the election of President and Vice President, to be electors appointed by a State; and they shall meet in the District and perform such duties as provided by the twelfth article of amendment.

Section 2.

The Congress shall have power to enforce this article by appropriate legislation.

Amendment XXIV
Passed by Congress August 27, 1962. Ratified January 23, 1964.

Section 1.

The right of citizens of the United States to vote in any primary or other election for President or Vice President, for electors for President or Vice President, or for Senator or Representative in Congress, shall not be denied or abridged by the United States or any State by reason of failure to pay poll tax or other tax.

Section 2.

The Congress shall have power to enforce this article by appropriate legislation.

Amendment XXV

Passed by Congress July 6, 1965. Ratified February 10, 1967.

Note: Article II, section 1, of the Constitution was affected by the 25th amendment.

Section 1.

In case of the removal of the President from office or of his death or resignation, the Vice President shall become President.

Section 2.

Whenever there is a vacancy in the office of the Vice President, the President shall nominate a Vice President who shall take office upon confirmation by a majority vote of both Houses of Congress.

Section 3.

Whenever the President transmits to the President pro tempore of the Senate and the Speaker of the House of Representatives his written declaration that he is unable to discharge the powers and duties of his office, and until he transmits to them a written declaration to the contrary, such powers and duties shall be discharged by the Vice President as Acting President.

Section 4.

Whenever the Vice President and a majority of either the principal officers of the executive departments or of such other body as Congress may by law provide, transmit to the President pro tempore of the Senate and the Speaker of the House of Representatives their written declaration that the President is unable to discharge the powers and duties of his office, the Vice President shall immediately assume the powers and duties of the office as Acting President.

Thereafter, when the President transmits to the President pro tempore of the Senate and the Speaker of the House of Representatives his written declaration that no inability exists, he shall resume the powers and duties of his office unless the Vice President and a majority of either the principal officers of the executive department or of such other body as Congress may by law provide, transmit within four days to the President pro tempore of the Senate and the Speaker of the House of Representatives their written declaration that the President is unable to discharge the powers and duties of his office.

Thereupon Congress shall decide the issue, assembling within forty-eight hours for that purpose if not in session. If the Congress, within twenty-one days after receipt of the latter written declaration, or, if Congress is not in session, within twenty-one days after Congress is required to assemble, determines by two-thirds vote of both Houses that the President is unable to discharge the powers and duties of his office, the Vice President shall continue to discharge the same as Acting President; otherwise, the President shall resume the powers and duties of his office.

Amendment XXVI
Passed by Congress March 23, 1971. Ratified July 1, 1971.

Note: Amendment 14, section 2, of the Constitution was modified by section 1 of the 26th amendment.

Section 1.

The right of citizens of the United States, who are eighteen years of age or older, to vote shall not be denied or abridged by the United States or by any State on account of age.

Section 2.

The Congress shall have power to enforce this article by appropriate legislation.

Amendment XXVII
Originally proposed September 25,1789. Ratified May 7, 1992.

No law, varying the compensation for the services of the Senators and Representatives, shall take effect, until an election of representatives shall have intervened.

Sources: http://www.foundingfathers.info/foundingdocuments/ The Bill of Rights and
http://www.foundingfathers.info/Other Amendments to the Constitution

Our Country is the United States of America.

We Love Our Country

Additional Sources

Coates, Sr., Eyler Robert (n.d.). *Jefferson on Politics & Government: Inalienable Rights.* Retrieved July 24, 2009 from http://etext.virginia.edu/jefferson/quotations.htm

EdWatch - Education for a Free Nation. *Curriculum Modules for Teachers.* Retrieved April 28, 2010 from http://www.edwatch.org

http://www.wallbuilders.com

_____. (n.d.). *Founding Documents.* Retrieved July 4, 2009 from

http://www.foundingfathers.info/Other founding documents:

The Declaration of Independence, The U.S. Constitution, The

Bill of Rights, and other Amendments to the Constitution, The

Federalist Papers Online

_____. (n.d.). *Natural and Legal Rights.* Retrieved

August 6, 2009 from

http://en.wikipedia.org/wiki/Inalienable_rights

93395308R00065

Made in the USA
Columbia, SC
11 April 2018